Ron Coleman William Ellis & Karen Taylor

Developing Peer Workers
A Working to Recovery Learning Manual

Copyright 2007
Published by P & P Press
ISBN 9781974279319

Developing Peer Support Workers

This manual is aimed at trainers who are delivering the "Developing Peer Workers" course produced by Working to Recovery This manual will provide you with the tools and knowledge you need to effectively develop peers in the workplace. It further explains the concepts and exercises held in the developing peers' course.

Essentials
During this week you will need some essential equipment. Below is a complete list of what to take with you or make sure it is accessible on the course.

1) Developing Peer Support Workers Workbooks. You will need to take enough for all the candidates and a few spare for emergencies, people will and do lose them so be prepared. You will also need this manual that you will use yourself.
2) Small note-books for everyone on the course.
3) Pens and pencils.
4) Board markers.

5) Access to an A-board, or
   alternatively take a large pad that
   can be displayed on the walls.
6) Envelopes for everyone.
7) Blue-tac
8) Post it notes

Table Of Contents

Introductions
Our Working Agreement
Getting to know you/A letter to me
Hopes fears and expectations
Introduction to the role
Why this training exists
Role-playing exercise
Respectful interactions
What brought you here?
Informal and formal peer support
The language of recovery
Intro to Respectful interactions
Role-playing exercise
Working from strengths
Communicating respectfully
Respecting differences.
Role-playing exercise
Recovery Environment
Who are you?
Diversity
Culture/Environment
New Outlook
A big mistake
Role modelling recovery
Our gifts
My story
Learning log

At the start of the week it is your responsibility to create as relaxed an atmosphere as possible, remember most people will be anxious about the intensity and content of the week ahead.

To create this comfort zone you need to continuously role model what a peer worker is and does from the very outset, which is based on the ethos of recovery. Throughout the week the environment will develop into one of recovery. This recovery environment is what makes the training so effectual. Those attending feel safe to divulge more about themselves while at the same time they contribute to the safety of others. You will have opportunities to highlight this to the group during the course.

Day 1

Before you get started, you need to introduce yourself to the people on the course. They will have the same opportunity soon. However as you; are the trainer it is only good practice that you role model recovery interactions. Introducing yourself should only take a few minutes but as with the rest of your participation, everything should be seen as an opportunity to further enhance the environment for recovery.
On this course you will be discovering more about yourself and the candidates, to this end your introduction starts the journey you will undertake over the coming week.

Below are some things you could speak about in your introduction.
1) The path that brought you to this place.
2) Some aspects of your own development.
3) What your expectations and fears for the week are.
4) Some of your own life history and experience.
5) Why you believe in this training.

Getting to Know You (1HOUR)

Now that you have introduced yourself it is time to find out a little about everyone else. We have made this part formulaic so as to lessen tensions about performance within the group. It is only natural that in large groups, some people will feel ill at ease. By making the exercise formulaic you direct the time it takes and the content that people divulge. You should ask everyone to split up into pairs and work from the Getting to Know You handout.

Explain a little to the trainees about how to fill in the form.

For instance where it states-
This person is originally from
It is up to the person filling it in to ask: "where are you from?" and then fill in the blank.
This exercise takes the form of an interview, where one person finds out specific things about the other and then feeds it back to the whole group. This exercise can take anything up to forty minutes depending on the size of the group.

TOP TIP

Throughout this manual we will offer some top tips that we have found help us to achieve our overall aim. As people are reading out the Getting to know you sheet, it is good practice to write down everyone's name and where they sit in the room. This will help you to speedily memorise who everyone is. By doing this you should be the first person in the room whose able to refer to others by their first name. This helps create connectivity and confidence within the group. The sooner you know everyone's name the better.

<u>Getting to know you.</u>

Please spend five minutes speaking to someone in the room that you don't know and fill in the blanks below.

Ladies and Gentlemen: It gives me great pleasure to introduce you to

(Full name)

__________________________________.

(First name)
(Birthplace)

____________________ **is originally from**

____________________.

(First name)
(Hometown)

____________________ **now lives in**
____________________ **and has done for ____ yrs.**

(First name)

If ____________________ was stranded on a desert island, the things they would

choose to take are: -

____

__________.

(First name)

_______________________s favourite film is

_______________________.

(First name)

If_______________________ **had some extra cash to use, their luxury item would**

be

_______________________.

(First name)

Something interesting about _______________________ **is** _______________________

____

_______________________.

(First name)

_______________________ **wants Peer Training because** _______________________

____

____

Our Working Agreement (1/2HOUR)

Before we embark on this, or any training we need to create a working agreement. This agreement functions on two levels. Firstly it creates positive boundaries within which the whole group can operate and secondly it can be used to heighten expectations of the week ahead. For instance, in your agreement you may express the desire for honesty within the group, when people undertake other courses being honest may not be a prerequisite set up by the people attending. The whole group should feel responsible for this agreement. To this end it is your role to let everyone contribute.

To achieve this you should check in with the whole group that they all agree that a suggestion should make it into the agreement.

As people call out what they would like in the agreement you should ask them for an example of what they mean and then write their suggestion on an A-board that will be on display throughout the week.

TOP TIP Give responsibility for the upkeep of the working agreement to the group. For example if timekeeping is on the list, then the group are responsible if it isn't being adhered to. Explain that you wont be acting like a head teacher and that working within the agreement is every persons' responsibility, as is updating it if need be.

Our Working Agreement

As we will be working closely and openly with each other over the next week, it is imperative that we lay some guiding principles that we all agree on. The content of this course lends to people being open and discussing personal experiences. To this end we should all feel safe.

With the agreement comes responsibility. We will all be responsible for implementing and keeping to it. In building this agreement you should consider what would help you keep safe. For instance the reassurance of privacy and confidentiality can be the cornerstone of any working agreement. Your final agreement will be on full view throughout this course. If at any point you feel the need for adjustments, then we will consider it as a group.

Below are some examples of what may make up your agreement.

1) Confidentiality. What is said in the room stays in the room.

2) Respect. One person speaks at a time and no one should be spoken over.

3) Timekeeping. We keep to the syllabus and the timescales.

4) Stay safe. Don't divulge personal information that you may not want to.

5) Tolerance. Don't jump to assumptions or make judgements about others.

6) Listen. Share the space equally

7) Be focussed. Don't stray onto other topics, stay in the discussion.

8) Participate. Speak up and become part of the discussions.

Our Working Agreement

Our working agreement will be on full view throughout this course. However you should keep a copy within this book. You may wish to refer back to it at any point so having it close to hand may be necessary. You will refer back to this book throughout the future and it can be beneficial to remind yourselves what priorities were set out at the beginning of this course and how they evolved to adapt to the group.

<table>
<tr><td align="center">Our Working Agreement</td></tr>
<tr><td>1)

2)

3)

4)

5)

6)</td></tr>
</table>

Now that we all know each other's names and we have laid down our working agreement, it is time for the course to start.

As recovery starts with self, and this course is designed for peer workers who can empathise rather than sympathise it is designed in such a way that people start to remember who they are, this in turn fosters recovery with the person they are working with. During this exercise the trainees will touch upon what brought them here. It is a self- reflective piece that starts the process of self- development.

TOP TIP We find that creating self-responsibility for what the trainees can achieve during the week fosters self-confidence.

This is why we ask the group to read the manual out loud as we work through it. Simply ask someone to start reading, when they feel they have read enough someone else will take over. Initially some people will feel self conscious about reading out loud, however as the week progresses it becomes second nature. There may be some long pauses between speakers and it may feel awkward. However by not trying to "fix it" and asking someone to read to you, you are modelling recovery.

Ask someone to start reading from their workbook. As you will be role modelling recovery this week it is your responsibility to complete the exercise first.

Write the three ages you have picked on the A-board and follow this with what you would tell yourself at these ages.
Now give the trainees five minutes to fill in their own.

Split the bigger group into four smaller groups and explain that they have ten minutes to consider what the benefits of self- reflection are.

TOP TIP It is beneficial for you to join the groups as they undertake discussions during the week. It helps to instil confidence in your abilities and you also get the opportunity to learn more about the people on the training. Move between the groups asking questions like

"What have we come up with?" or "How are we getting on?"

However do not take responsibility for any group you are in. You should be more of a helpful observer.
The trainees are now ready to write themselves a letter.

Explanations for this exercise are on the handout; however you should expand upon these. Everyone should take ten minutes and write a letter to them selves. These should be placed in the envelopes provided, upon which everyone needs to write their own name.

You will collect all the letters in now and keep them in a safe place.

The letters will be delivered to the person at the end of the course

When you have completed this weeks training, your trainee's will realise the potential they have within. The course is designed in such a way that not only will they be able to further enhance someone else's recovery journey, but fundamentally, they will further develop and evolve with their own recovery.

This is the essence of recovery, the YO-YO principle

You Own Your Own!

Next Exercise, (please do this exercise on your self as well)
You can then walk alongside others carrying the hope. At times it can be difficult to step back and reflect honestly upon the strengths we carry. This can be the difference between a peer support specialist and other workers in the mental health field. We are always acknowledging and working from people's strengths and potential, this starts with your own. As part of your continuing growth it is helpful to check in and realise how far you have come in relation to your own strengths, expectations and self-esteem.

Imagine if you will, as part of your own journey you could travel back in time to give out some insightful knowledge, what would you say to 15 year old you?

"Never take the advice of someone who has not had your kind of trouble." Sidney J. Harris

Would you give out advice?

Tell them to apply for a position; you now regret not going for?

Tell them not to be scared?

Tell them not to hide their light under a bushel?

Tell them to take more risks?

Point out some pitfalls in the future?

Maybe let them know that things will all work out ok in the long
Run?

During this next exercise we will remember ourselves at three different ages.

Please record in your workbooks
Age _______

You should know that
Age _______

You should know that
Age _______

You should know that let's now imagine
that the reverse is true.
If the past you could speak to the present
you what things would you say. You
should all relish the opportunity of
travelling back in time and giving
yourselves advice. Unfortunately it is
impossible.

But wouldn't it be great!

However communicating with the future
you is completely achievable!

How so? You might ask.

Well if we can take the time to develop our
own plans, we can certainly take the time
to let ourselves know of our fears, hopes

and trepidations. It may seem like a pointless task to inform ourselves about how we feel, however we grow and flourish in the recovery process by understanding both who we are and how we got there.

Lori Ashcroft defines this quite eloquently with her description of recovery.

"Recovery is remembering who you are and using your strengths to become all you were meant to be"

Without going into the tools we can utilise for this purpose, let's first as a whole group discuss the benefits of being able to hear our voice from the past.

In groups discuss the benefits of reflecting on who we were and how this influences us now. Please record in your workbooks
Please make some photocopies of letter below to hand out to trainee's

A letter to me.

Now that we have looked at, and discussed the potential to grow from self-reflection, it is time to put it into practice.

It's always nice to get a letter from someone we love. Use the tear off piece below and write a letter to yourself. It will then be delivered to you, by the Working to Recovery Postal Service at the end of the course. Tell yourself how you are feeling. What is going on with you at the moment? What are your fears and expectations for the week ahead, what will the training mean for you in the long term? Just the type of thing you may send to a loved one far from home.

- - - - -

Dear ___________

____

____

____

____

____

____

____

____

____

____

____

____

Yours Sincerely _______________

Hopes, fears and expectations

The majority of learning and discovery for the people on this course is experiential. By the end of the week everyone will have experienced what it is to work within a recovery environment. It is this same environment that they will be expected to go into the workplace and re-create. To this end you should continuously highlight some of the changes that you have noticed taking place during the week. For instance if someone has to leave the room for whatever reason it is worth pointing out how the climate changes without them. As the environment develops the trainees need to be able to reflect on how this happened. One of the main aspects of this course is recognising people's strengths and how we can cope in stressful and difficult situations. When they read their letters they will be surprised at how far they have come in regards to their own self-confidence .We have included lots of exercises and group work that will give people on the course the capacity to recognise their own strength and remember how to feel proud of themselves. This is why we now look at all of our fears, hopes and expectations for the week ahead.

Again this piece of work is self-explanatory see the handout on next page.

Ask the group to split into pairs and discuss their own fears, hopes and expectations for the week ahead.

After ten minutes you should get everyone back together in the big group and ask people to read out their conclusions.

Write up what is said on the A-board, explaining that it will be on view for the entire week

<u>Handout</u>

Hopes, Fears and Expectations

Before we embark on what will be an exciting journey of peer support training, it is important for us, as a group to be able to look back and reflect upon what expectations we came with. At the beginning of any journey we all have hopes and concerns for the path ahead. Whether they are fears of fitting in, or we may not feel that we are up to the challenge. As a peer support worker acknowledging our strengths and the strengths of others is an imperative part of our roles. Everyone should take ten minutes working with a partner to discuss what are their hopes, fears and expectations for the week ahead. Our own hopes, fears and expectations should be kept in our work-books and revisited during the course. We will discuss them in depth with the bigger group, looking further into whether they will be met during our time together.

HOPES

EXPECTATIONS   FEAR

TOP TIP As you scribe on the A-board the feedback from the groups' hopes, fears and expectations, for instance someone may say that they expect to be able to be in a better position to help the people they work with. You could go onto explain that this course is focused on self. That recovery workers role model the ethos and to this end they will not get a formulated check list of things to undertake which means they are working in recovery. However they will learn how to connect with themselves and this in turn will help them connect with the person

<u>Introduction to the role</u>

This part of the course gives background to the role of peer workers. At working to recovery we believe that someone with a mental health diagnosis need not necessarily fill the peer role. It is our contention that understanding recovery is to understand human condition. Peer support has taken off around the world and some organisations will only employ a peer on the basis of a diagnosis.

As this course is about self-development and recovery starts with self it seems defeating to base the role in a diagnosis that someone else gives them. During the week people will start to remember who they are and begin the journey of self-development. Some people will have personal issues that they may need to re-examine. This is where this course works on many levels, it is remembering the times when the participants over came major hurdles that helped them to carry the hope for others. The trainees will start to realise that just as they came through tough times so too will the people they work with.

What is Peer Support and can it happen?

Jim Burdett the managing director of Mind and Body Consultants Ltd in New Zealand describes peer support in the following way.
"The term "Peer Support" describes an equal and supportive relationship based on common experience. Mental illness can produce crippling feelings of isolation, stigma and shame. One way to alleviate these feelings is to let people know that they are not alone – that they have peers with similar experiences who have recovered to lead worthwhile and enjoyable lives." In essence then peer support requires the involvement of someone who has had mental health problems of their own and has now recovered. They then use their recovery experience to help other people with mental health problems get their lives back.
The Recovery Education Centre run by Meta Service Inc describes Peer support as "A journey that leads to knowing how to take all of your experiences, regardless of the pain and use them to transform our

life into what we call 'living hope' for others who want to recover."

<u>Why does this training exist?</u>

At working to Recovery we have always worked from the view that the person is the expert of their own experience. Peer support workers utilise this expertise when walking alongside others on their recovery journeys. Our aim is not to show people how to recover. Rather to support them in undertaking their own journey, as we have.

Recovery should no longer be an "add on" extra permitted to the privileged few. Working to Recovery believe, recovery should be a fundamental right open to everyone. Peer support training brings together many threads of practice that we have been providing worldwide for many years. We provide many courses on recovery, hearing voices and self-harm. We have been instrumental in supporting major organisations undertake recovery as their core ethos. Through peer support training we are uniting these threads and directing them straight into the practice of recovery. At this point in the day it is good practice to take five minutes for a group discussion. As a trainer in recovery and peer working you will be role modelling the ethos of recovery continuously. You should always pre-empt some parts of the training that follow later in the week. Now is a perfect opportunity to role model recovery interactions. You should listen reflectively to what the group have to say and respond with open-ended questions. At the end of the week when people are reflecting on what happened you will be able to highlight your own practice and remind them that you have been utilising recovery interactions throughout the course. They will remember when you have and realise that they too can perform these same interactions.

TOP TIP when creating an environment for recovery we need to create some breathing space. As the trainer you will be continuously monitoring the group looking for signals that let you know people are uncomfortable. If you are picking up on some people feeling uneasy it is good practice to stop and have a small discussion about what we have covered or find out if people have some burning questions. There are some parts of this workbook that people can work through in

their own time and this is where you can
create space.

What is Peer Support? (3/4 Hour)
There are a number of ways in which we can define peer support,
Defining Peer Support
The purpose of the following exercise is to find out what participants believe peer support is. It is important that from the very beginning of a training session participants are encouraged to think about the meaning of the topic. The exercise is designed to encourage this process.

The exercise
Before starting the exercise proper everyone should have a post-it and a pen. Guide them to take three minutes to think about how they would define peer support and then to write on a post-it. Once they have written their definition everyone will share their definition with the whole group and then stick the post-it on the sheet provided. As the facilitator you should consider and explore not only the differences but also the commonalities that are held by people about peer support. It is okay to change their definition of peer support throughout the course of the week and if they do, they should write it on a post-it putting the post-it on the " what is peer support sheet".

The Elements of Peer Support

The purpose of this exercise is to explore the diverse elements that are involved in the peer support process.

The Exercise

For this exercise they should work in pairs it is often useful to work with someone they do not know. Once they have paired up, they should talk to each other about a time they received peer support. This could be anything, a cold, a broken leg, a relationship break-up, bereavement, a pregnancy or even a breakdown. They should take turns to speak for ten minutes about their experience and their partner should note what the key elements of peer support for them were. Everyone will feedback to the main group the main elements of peer support and these should be noted on the flipchart. Once these elements are recorded you will address the following question with them.

What do you think the key elements of peer support would be in mental health?

When we look to the past for evidence of formal peer support, there are three predominant eras in which the concept and use of peer support specialists has been utilised. The first sat alongside the practice of Philippe Pinel. Pinel was born in France 1745. He studied medicine and became interested in mental health after a friend of his committed suicide while receiving treatment for "nervous melancholy"

He believed the treatment directly influenced his friends' death and sought to make changes in practice and the way people with mental health problems were treated. He gained employment at the Bicetre Hospital in Paris under the tutelage of Jean Baptise Pussin. Pussin had implemented non-violent and non medical treatments which came to be known as "moral treatment" Pinel took this moral treatment further and eradicated the use of bleeding, purging and blistering; instead focusing on close contact and observations of patients. Pinel believed the best people to understand and empathise with people undergoing mental health problems were those who had had similar experiences. Hence he employed nurses who had recovered from experiences of their own. The main role these peer nurses fulfilled was that of understanding the experience and being capable of supporting others through their problems rather than becoming a recipient of medical care.

The second arose as a result of international loss of identity during the great depression. The Great Depression was a worldwide economic downturn which started in October of 1929 and lasted through most of the 1930s. It began in the United States and quickly spread to Europe and every part of the world, with devastating effects in industrialised countries. Cities all around the world were hit hard, especially those based on heavy industry. Unemployment and homelessness soared.
 Men who had previously been in full time employment found that their circumstances had changed practically overnight. The security held within a full time skilled post was destroyed; furthermore they had no other posts to fill

as the eradication of jobs spread like a chain reaction.

With the loss of jobs came the loss of hope and self purpose. A full time job takes up almost all of our waking week, so the sudden loss of this purposeful role can be a heavy burden to carry. Many men found some solace in the company of others partaking in alcohol. This sudden rise in a drinking culture resulted in further eradication of peoples lives. Not only had they lost their jobs but now they had acquired addictions and the chaotic lifestyles that can come with them.

People with alcohol addiction could not afford the treatments of the day so they turned to other means of creating their own social and personnel recovery. This was initiated through the inception of alcoholics anonymous. The A.A. was started by two alcoholics who first met on May 12, 1935. One was Bill Wilson, a New York Wall Street stock speculator; the other was Dr. Bob Smith, a medical doctor and surgeon from Akron, Ohio. In A.A. circles, the former is known as "Bill W." and the latter, "Dr. Bob." Wilson had been sober for six months when he met Smith, although he had struggled with sobriety for years. From those experienced in recovery by religious means, Wilson had learned from the opinion of famed psychiatrist Dr. Carl G. Jung that alcoholism could be cured by a genuine conversion rather than medical intervention or other therapeutic means. The AA devised the now famous twelve-step programme, which is one of the first forms of person cantered planning. Now there existed an organization where people who had experience of an addiction supported and stood alongside people undergoing similar experiences. When undertaking the twelve-step program the person is allocated a "sponsor", the sponsor has been through the program themselves and stands alongside to offer support for the person. This is a fundamental part of peer support.

The third is found in today's climate of recovery.

It is only in the past twenty or so years that stories of personal journeys have come to the fore in the world of psychiatry; before this people relied on case studies from psychiatrists to find solutions to personal problems. This resulted in people receiving treatments that may not have been tailored to their specific needs. As more stories of recovery emerged it became obvious that every person's journey is unique but built on similar foundations of hope, belief and understanding. The problem with a medical model is that its aim is to fix people. With the advent of recovery people now build their own plans and work from their own strengths. As more and more people undertook their recovery it became clear that they could in turn support others undergoing similar experiences. This led to the formation of self help groups and peer driven services. There are many examples of current peer driven services some of which being Mind, Body and Soul, Wellink, AMH's, and the Lighthouse in New Zealand and META services in the USA. The main drive behind all peer support is that the person is an expert through experience.

<u>Informal and Formal Peer Support (1/4 hour)</u>

When looking for support from others we may have many avenues open to us. For instance when seeking advice, a professional may not be best placed to fulfil our unique needs. Would it be reasonable to approach a relationship counsellor whenever we have an argument with our partner? A professional can help when we need someone who is objective and outside our realm. However the majority of our challenges can be dealt with through a close network of people who will understand the nuances of the situation we are in. You may have many people in your life whom will carry out the function of, informal peer support and in turn you will form part of other people's network of informal peer support.

Informal peer groups can be found wherever people meet. Pubs are full of small peer groups, which form part of the larger group in the pub. Informal peers are those we communicate equally with on an almost daily basis. Informal peers can and do offer us some guidance and support however they are not obliged to, we seek them out and they may not even know they are helping.

Exercise

As a group you will generate a list of formal and informal peers on an A-board. Use the workbooks provided to write down the group's conclusions.

What makes an informal peer?

What makes a formal peer?

What can the benefits of these groups be?

Formal Peers

Would you like to see services that you are involved with adopt formal peer support?

If so, how can you help to enable the process?

Formal peers work within the constraints of guidelines and at times policies. They have an objective to work to and that is why we seek them out. They may be paid for the expertise they have gained in a certain area. For instance people who work at the Lighthouse in New Zealand can only be employed if they have been through what has been considered to be a severe psychosis. This makes them an expert by experience. Other formal peers groups may be organisations like the hearing voices network or even a local credit union. This is one of the fundamental differences in formal and informal, the first provides specific expertise that we can utilise and may be paid for providing this service. The latter may range from a close friend to someone we infrequently meet in the pub.

So far we have covered a lot of ground in a short period of time. Again this is a perfect opportunity to check in and role model recovery. Take ten minutes for a group discussion. During this discussion you should be using recovery interactions while recapping what the group have covered. Now we have covered the history of peer support, the elements and what peer support is.

It is time to step up a gear. This next exercise is designed to highlight how we all interact with each other based on the relationship and trust we hold and this will decide how much information we are willing to divulge. The trainees will come to their own conclusions as to how much information they want everyone else to know about them.

The purpose of this exercise is two-fold.

Firstly it highlights what it must be like for a person using a service where everyone knows their life history, and whether this life history is in fact a true reflection of what has happened. Secondly it gets the trainees thinking about how they may have compartmentalised their life so far and why.

TOP TIP. This is the start of the trainees recovery journey therefore you should allow people as much time as possible to fill in their timeline- a way of expressing your life story in diagram form. When they have completed the exercise it is the perfect time to speak about the "WHO AM I?" Exercise tomorrow. Briefly explain that they will be presenting on who they are for five minutes tomorrow but we will cover the subject in greater detail before the end of the session.

What brought you here? (3/4 hour)

When you become a peer support specialist, one of the recovery tools you will be proficient in using is listening and developing a persons life story or personal narrative. As with all journeys, your journey into peer support had a beginning. That is what we will now explore, the beginning of this journey. Work in pairs discussing the main events in your life that you consider to have been instrumental to bringing you on this course. You should mark these points off on a time line of your own please look at positive as well as negative parts of your journey. We will be delving deeper into our own journeys during this course and furthermore asking the question

"Who am I?"

Ask the participants to fill in the time line in their workbooks it will look like this below. Fill this in for yourself

My Timeline

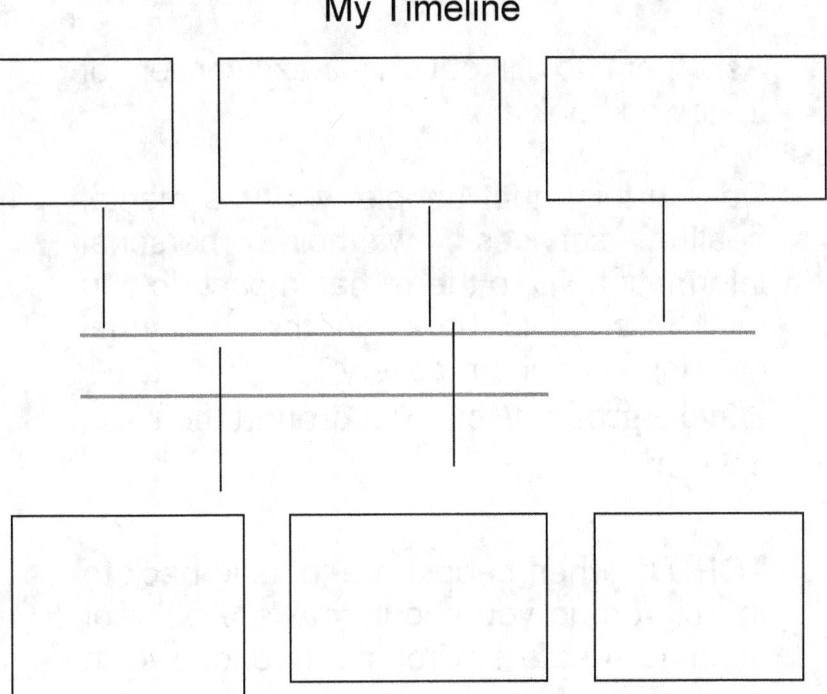

After each person chooses another person from the group to share their story with, discussing the significant times in their life, ask them to spend ten minutes alone reading over what they have placed in the text boxes. Were these events really the

times in their life that re-directed and sent them on different paths? Were these the most significant and meaningful events that have left a lasting impact? If not, ask them to take the time to consider why they all might hold back telling someone about themselves.

Ask them to fill out this next section of their workbook

Do you think that people who use mental health services withhold personal information? if so then what impact do you think this could have on their personal development and recovery?
Have a group discussion around their answers.

TOP TIP when people are feeding back to the big group you should make a point of creating a safe environment conducive to disclosure. Make sure all mobiles are switched off and ask anyone if they need to leave the room for any reason, to do so now.
Do not start the feedback until you are sure that no one will be interrupted.

Recovery and Rocket Science

For many years we have heard speakers and trainers in the mental health field comparing the simplicity of recovery to rocket science.
"This isn't rocket science"
They mean the concept, or practice they are working from is easy to understand and implement, unlike rocket science. The truth is that mental health practice and ideology are incomparable to any form of linear, scientific, factual based practice. Unlike rocket science, the art of supporting someone on their own recovery journey is different every time we work with someone. If you build one rocket from scientific principals, then you will be able to replicate your results time and time again, however just because one person diagnosed with Bi-polar disorder has some plans that work for them does not mean they will work for anyone else. Rocket science is a precise and technical based practice which has its roots in over a thousand years of development, whereas psychiatry as we know it is in its infancy. It

is only in the last century that we have seen the development of diagnosis, medication, psycho-analysis, psycho-dynamics, CBT, REBT, MBT etc, Although rocket science may be highly technical and engulfed in complicated equations it never the less has specific laws within which it works. This is the fundamental difference between psychiatry and other sciences. Psychiatry is based on constructs whereas other sciences are rooted in observable truths, such as physics and electronics. As a peer support specialist there are techniques that you can hone to the best of you're ability but you must always work with someone in a way that is unique to them.

You will always work from the standpoint that

The person is the expert of their own experience.

To this end, we no longer work with a diagnosis or labels rather we work with the person. This is implicit in all of our interactions.

"You cannot acquire experience by making experiments. You cannot create experience. You must undergo it."

Albert Camus (1913 - 1960)

If you are delivering this training as a one-week course, we have now reached the end of day one.

You should take this time to recap with the group what has been discussed and whether the working agreement has been adhered to. This is when you will fully explain what the "Who am I?" presentations tomorrow will look like. Explain that everyone will present to the bigger group for five minutes on who they are.

Who they are is not the roles they perform on a daily basis. They should stay clear of speaking about being a mother or brother or support worker. The aim of this exercise is to get people remembering who they are. Make a note of the order in which they will be presenting. On day two you can allocate the time for these presentations in two different ways. Use up a block of time and get everyone to do theirs at the same time, or just ask during the day if people are ready to do theirs yet.

Notes

DAY 2

It is good working practice to start the day with a discussion of what took place on the previous day. Again refer to the working agreement and discuss how the environment has changed compared to yesterday morning.

Today people will be presenting their "who am I?"
When people are presenting you should make sure they have no interruptions and the room feels safe. The total time taken up on day two for these presentations will be roughly 1-2 hours, depending on how many trainees there are.

Now that the trainees have started their own recovery journeys we will begin to work on good practices. It is very probable that the trainees have been referring to people who use services as clients, tenants, patients and service users rather than person first language. You should now bring to their attention that you don't refer to people as categories and everyone you speak to understands what you are saying.

TOP TIP Do not, under any circumstances refer to any of the trainees language so far. As with all recovery it is not your position to fix how they refer to people but rather to show them positive alternatives.

The Language of Recovery (1 hours including)

As Peer specialists we may have experienced stigma and discrimination at different points on our journeys. To this end it is within our role to lead by example. As a peer specialist in the mental health field you will understand the effect that stigma and discrimination can have on someone's recovery. The world of mental health uses clinical language that can be overpowering and at times is impenetrable. For instance you may hear people being referred to through their diagnosis. i.e. So and so is a "schizophrenic", or "He's a cutter"

Or we come across a scientific language that sounds like a mix between the scripts of ER and Star Trek. "The haloperidol the CPN administers is working more effectively than the Olanzapine, but the chance of Tardive Dyskinesia is a trade off against the schizo- effective disorder"

If you are looking for the letters Z, Y, X and Q and are wondering how they are put to use in the English language, look no further than Psychiatry. Recovery short-circuits this medical language as we work with the person rather than a diagnosis. We interact mutually and respectfully and to this end the language we use presents our underlying ethos. As a peer specialist you will be working from people's strengths rather than concentrating on what they cannot do. We use person first language that is natural and specific to people's experiences.

"Grasp the subject, the

words will follow."

Cato the Elder (234 BC - 149 BC)

<u>Strong Recovery language</u>
In your groups you should read these descriptions of maintenance language. Use the space provided in your workbooks to transform them into strong Recovery language.
1) Peter is a schizophrenic
2) Susan is paranoid.
3) Joan is non compliant about her medication.
4) John is delusional and there is no point talking to him.
5) He's always suicidal
6) Paul is always bouncing back to hospital
7) Joanne thinks she can win X factor
8) Watch out for Jim when he has no fags left. He becomes manipulative.
9) Jane is continuously annoying her GP about her condition.
10) Henry is being persecuted by his voices.
11) Patricia has no insight into her illness.
12) Fred's self harm is just a cry for attention.
13) Ross medication makes him lazy
14) Stuart can't talk to new people.
15) He needs his cash budgeted or else he just spends it.

16) Victoria always becomes depressed at Christmas.
17) Annabel has never had a job.
18) Because Steven is a drug addict his GP will no longer prescribe him Valium.
 19) Vince brings attention to himself in public by talking to his voices.

"You must continue to gain expertise, but avoid thinking like an expert."
Waitley, Denis

<u>Respectful Interactions(1 ½ hours)</u>

When working as a peer support specialist it is essential that we understand the impact that respect and mutuality can bring to our relationships, in the workplace and also in our personal lives. When people have been diagnosed with a mental health problem, it can be easier for staff to relate all of the person's reactions back to the diagnosis rather than to the person's experience. For instance when someone becomes tearful or reacts angrily to a certain situation, the anger can be seen as part of the symptoms of the illness rather than a reaction to the situation they were in. When people are viewed through a diagnosis it can be difficult for staff to get beyond the "fix them" syndrome. When we work in a mutual and respectful way, we respect and acknowledge the person's resilience and strength in being able to express them selves. Rather than seeing someone through the lens of maintenance, we can further enhance the persons' journey of recovery by being wholly with them during expressive times, this is a skill which peer support specialists need to fine tune. This is achieved with practice and lots of feedback. Working mutually also allows us to grow and develop as co-learners with the person with whom we are working. Many of us have learned that supporting someone in mental health services is a way of using our expertise. However with recovery and working as a peer support specialist, you will recognise that the person is the expert of their own experience. People who are supported can be seen as "less capable". Most of us have been supported and received help from professionals, who are viewed as experts that benefited us and helped us on our own journeys. Such as GPs, therapists, social workers etc, they are experts by professional knowledge! Not by experience. We will also have received help from professionals that weren't very helpful at all. Professional relationships can be beneficial when they are based in recovery. That is; we are respected and listened to and our needs are taken into consideration. When there is recognition that both parties bring an expertise it can make the relationship more effective. As a peer support specialist you will understand that everyone has the best possible knowledge about them selves. This in turn leads to them directing the service they receive. Every person is treated with respect and dignity, regardless of whether they use services or not. When we work from a mutual platform we understand that we are not "better" than the person we support. We are open to learning and growing from them. As a peer you will work alongside someone who will direct their own journey, as they know what is best for them and where they want to go.

We have started the process of working from good recovery practice.
Now we will put it to the test. This next exercise is one that we will visit every day. Some trainees feel awkward in role-playing exercises. This is why we have personalised it. Again you should role model and lead from the outset. Take ten minutes to undertake the exercise yourself before the group have a go.

Exercise (1hour)
In groups of three you will read a short role-playing exercise. Try out a respectful and dignified interaction, focussing in on a time in your life where you faced some challenge. One person will act as the peer support specialist the other will make

some specific notes on their observations of the interaction. Each will take a turn at each role. The person observing needs to remain neutral throughout. Remember this may be the first time someone has been put in the position of supporting another. To this end our overall objective is to highlight the peer workers strengths. This is a major stepping-stone. As a peer support specialist you will utilise the art of building a persons self -esteem by recognition of their strengths and gifts extensively throughout your work practice. It is important that you practice and reflect upon your own strengths regularly and extensively as well.

Scene one

You have been receiving support for over six months. It is Wednesday morning and as has been arranged, your worker is visiting you at home. Think of a time when you faced a challenge and could have used support For instance maybe losing a job or a break up in a relationship. Explain to your worker what has happened.

As the group learn more about creating an environment for recovery, we should take the time to reflect on what has been happening for everyone. Now is the time to get feedback on how everyone interacted during the role-playing exercise. Everyone should have a feedback form regarding another person in the group. During the feedback your role is to highlight all of the recovery practice that is taking place. You can also direct the feedback in such a way that the person giving the support is left with a feeling of achievement. The group will visit this exercise again. Highlight where people have been able to sit back and listen to the person without jumping in to fix the situation.

The healing within

The aim of this part of the course is to reiterate that as recovery workers we do not "recover people" This can be quite an enlightening part to the course as we have found the trainees find it liberating. As the trainer you will be able to refer back to this part of the course throughout the week. Whenever someone tries to solve a problem for someone else in the group you can remind them that they are trying to fix it for their own reasons.

When we jump in to "fix" people we rob them of the opportunity to grow and flourish. Always being on hand with advice can strengthen the maintenance model they have been engulfed in. As with our own lives, it can be more beneficial to learn from our own mistakes. Through this people will find their own ways of coping. People need to find their own solutions and build their own paths on their journey. To this end, being a peer specialist means we do not jump in at the first opportunity to try and "fix" a situation. We do not instantly offer advice that may have worked for us. We sit comfortably with the person, in a safe environment where they can work their way to personal solutions. This builds self-confidence. It may even be the first time that someone has felt allowed to own their own potential and show just how creative they can be. As someone works towards unravelling their own solutions, it is the peer specialist's role to be fully present and help to build on their belief that they will succeed. We do this using interaction's that re-enforce our belief in the person. Below is a list of some recovery -focussed interactions. These will form the basis of how we interact mutually throughout this course.

Working from strengths. (1hour)

The message underlying this part of the course will not be new to people. However the difference lies in vocalising what the person's strength is rather than building plans around them. Throughout the day you will have been acknowledging strengths and the trainees will have noticed. They should feel awkward the first time they practice but this will become second nature by the end of the week. The aim of this part is to get the trainees away from focusing on a diagnosis and to start working with the person. As a peer support specialist this will become second nature. When validating strengths we are re-affirming the person's potential to grow and learn. When we embark on our recovery journeys, we all need the strength that will see us through. At times we can receive this strength from others. We may have grown accustomed to feeling helpless and at other times we cannot see the wood for the trees. This is why it is important to highlight people's strengths, not only is it encouraging it is also spirit lifting and helps us to remember who we are. When we identify someone's strengths they in turn can learn to recognise the power that lies within. Below is the first exercise in validating strengths. We will be revisiting this many times during the week. Turn the scenario into a sentence whereby you are validating the person's strength. Please fill in this section of your workbook

1) John is refusing to take his medication, as he does not agree with his consultant.

2) Peter has self- referred to the crisis service for the fourth time.
3) Sheila puts her family first even when this may cause her distress.
4) Brendan has trouble holding down a job. In the past year he has been a salesman, a caretaker and a car mechanic.
5) William can overspend his entire monthly budget. This has left him far from home with no bus fare at times.
6) Susan has recently suffered a relapse and has re entered hospital.

Communication exercise.

Now that we are working on communication skills you should highlight for the trainees what poor communication looks like. Use post it notes and write the name of famous figures on them. Go around the room and put one on everyone's back. No one is to tell the person whom they are supposed to be. Now split the group into pairs and using questions that can only be answered with yes or no, they have to discover who they are.

This should take twenty minutes. The objective is to show the trainees that when we ask the person we work with closed questions they can forget who they are. When we ask open-ended questions they can start to remember who they are and build self-confidence from it.

TOP TIP If anyone discovers who they are quickly you should let the whole group know. You will be role modelling what it is to recognise strengths and how easy it can be with practice.

Communicating respectfully

Some relationships can become stale and we can almost predict what someone's responses might be. This in no way encourages recovery. When people are able to find their own solutions they can start to realise that they have the power of self-healing. At times we fall into "auto-pilot". Our interactions become jaded and there can be a tendency to go over old ground. Peer support specialists do not dominate conversations, on the contrary, people will be used to others offering advice and telling them the "right" thing to do. We listen to the person and create an environment where they can discover their own solutions. Sometimes we may communicate in a way that helps the person to tell us who they are and what they need. Being too overbearing negates this and fails to help the person grow. There is also the danger that someone will find it difficult to open up when we are overbearing. Ask the trainees go to the part of the workbook which looks at closed questions /open questions as below ask them to fill in the blanks using open ended questions that will help the person to discover their own solutions.

Are you distressed?	How are you feeling?
Would you rather be somewhere else?	How would you like this to be different?
Are you in a crisis?	What is going on at the moment?
Where you responsible?	Can you let me know what happened?
Are you coming later?	
Did you take your meds?	
Have you seen your consultant?	

Listening skills.

As a peer support specialist it is important to continually develop our communication skills. One of which is the sensitive use of reflective listening. As with "open ended" questions this skill can be difficult to master but the benefits for the person are returned ten fold. The skill held in "Peer "talk" is that we don't overuse any one tool. It would be disadvantageous to overly use reflective listening skills, as the person would feel like you have an agenda and don't really care about them. During our communications with someone we may just check in with them to confirm what we have heard. This is productive on two levels. It lets the person know we are listening and also we may have picked them up wrong or misunderstood what they where saying. To this end it points us in the right direction and lets the person know that we understand them fully. Reflective listening helps to set the pace of the conversation. We can slow something down a bit if we feel it is starting to go off at a tangent and then re-focus on the topic at hand. The most important point behind reflective listening is that the person gets a feel that we care about what they are saying to us. Here are some of the fundamentals of reflective listening: -

1) Avoid being judgemental, both in content and tone.
2) Do not over reflect. It becomes transparent that you are working from an agenda.
3) Continually assess the need for reflection.
4) Work with the rhythm of the conversation. Wait for pauses or create space for breathing and reflecting.
5) Do not over complicate things.
6) Practice! It looks easy but isn't.

Reflective listening examples

The conversation	Reflective statement
Peter is telling you that his relationship with his nurse is always one sided. He expresses his anger at her always thinking she knows what is best for him. He is thinking of complaining about her, but thinks it will be futile as she will blame him, as she always does.	" I can hear how upset you feel about this" Or "So its difficult to relate to your nurse"
Susan is moving town and has mixed feelings about the whole thing. She is moving so that she can study at a local college. However she will have to find a new GP.	"You're excited about the course but apprehensive about finding a GP as good as the one you have now"

The content of our reflective listening can get across a message of understanding, empathy and affirming. Here are some examples of reflective listening statements. Ask trainees to place them in the column in their workbooks that best describes what message it relates to the person.

1) "I think that takes a lot of courage"
2) "I have down days too."
3) "So you think it's the consultants fault."
4) "I think that shows a lot of guts".
5) "I remember being in a similar position.
6) "That is some journey. You must be really strong."
7) "Yes, I can see how that would work."
8) "We've spoken about your Story, discussed your new plans and you are looking forward to the future."
9) "I think it's great that you're looking at alternatives."
10) "So now you are using a dosage of medication that works for you and this has encouraged you to start thinking about employment."
11) "I love Dylan Thomas too."
12) "Sometimes it can seem difficult to express our feelings. I have the same trouble."

13) "You wrote to your consultant and when you get a response you will take it from there. I wish I had done that when I went through a similar experience. I think that's very creative."

Respecting differences.
As a peer support specialist you will be highlighting and role modelling recovery. It is our work ethic. As an expert of recovery you too will lead by example. We never get into a negative argument with someone we are working with, not only is it unprofessional it also reaffirms the maintenance model. We can put forward alternative views this should be done in a way that maintains a positive relationship. We respect fully the people we work with and remember that ultimately we are equally "experts in our own experience." In recovery we see resistance as a healthy positive indicator that recovery is taking place. If you meet someone week in and week out and their outlook and attitude is always the same then they may be stuck in maintenance. This is unhealthy. If someone has become distant and submissive it is your role to create a safe environment where they can express honestly how they are feeling. Again this

helps someone remember who they are and builds self confidence. When we encounter resistance we do not try to overwhelm the person with arguments, facts and experience.

We flow with them by listening and honouring their judgement. As a group we will look at the following scenario and find a way for James to roll with the resistance. James is a peer support specialist who is undertaking some wellness training for a group of 20 support workers.
Ian has been with the same organisation for 11 years and feels that he can learn nothing from today, as recovery is just a "buzz word" that will pass like all other fads.
James: " Can we split into two groups please and discuss the benefits of recovery as opposed to maintenance. Take 5 minutes and we'll hear from both groups in turn about what we can do today to change our approach."
Ian: "Why don't you just tell us, rather than wasting our time? If you know all the answers then get straight to it. I've got people to support. They need me more than I need this." Ask people to fill in the

next statement by James in to their workbook

James: Well, Ian ....

As a peer support specialist they will reflect their positive outlook and reinforce the hope they hold that not only do people recover but that they can achieve their dreams. The role brings with it some challenging aspects. For instance when creating an environment for recovery and utilising the safe area created, people will talk about what may be considered to be upsetting. However this is different to getting stuck in a problem. Our role is not to fix peoples situations, but rather to facilitate them creating and working towards their own solutions. We don't become stuck in a situation, or agree with someone because it is the easy thing to do.

Here is a brief example
A team mate: "My manager is useless. He doesn't understand the rota. He doesn't know what service we provide and he is so out of touch that he should just move on. I have been trying to get on some hearing voices training that will help me

work with someone but he says I don't need it. He is really starting to affect me."
Your reply:
"I can hear that you are frustrated and upset. How about we look at other ways of you getting what you need. Let's take a look at your options."
In this response we have fulfilled some basics in peer support. We recognised how the person is feeling. We let them know that we understand they have a problem, we encouraged them to take ownership and work towards a solution. Here is an example of what you should avoid saying in the above response.

"Yes, he sounds useless. You have every right to be upset just as we all do when we come across these people. I'll tell you about the manager I had that acted in the same way."

This is negative and reduces the possible outcomes.
- It encourages helplessness.
- It devolves responsibility.
- It encourages further negativity without looking for solutions.

Now is a good time to check in with the group. You should acknowledge some of the trainees' strengths and thank them for their contribution so far. Have a group discussion based on what they have covered so far. Some topics you can cover are.

- *Why is working from the point of view of a diagnosis detrimental to your relationship with the person.*
- *Cover what happened during writing their own timelines.*

TOP TIP All of your interactions with the group help build a recovery environment. It is good practice to check whether the working agreement is being followed and whether it needs to be amended. This helps you check in with how comfortable people are feeling This part of the training gives the trainees the tools to create and work within a recovery environment. We will now look at how to get our point heard while respecting a differing opinion from someone else. Before you begin this part you should split the group into pairs. Ask one person to face the wall and the other to stand behind them. The person standing behind them will tell them what strengths they have seen in the person facing the wall. This should take one minute and then ask them to change positions and repeat.

After this the trainees will be feeling a little elated and or embarrassed, its good to be told good things about our selves. Now highlight the difference between the aura in the room and what it feels like to work in a hostile environment.
This will create a short group discussion that will lead into the next part. The aim of this part of the course is to get the trainees practising disagreeing with others without it escalating into an argument.

A positive disagreement.

It is perfectly reasonable to disagree with the person you are working with. We don't just plod along with people, agreeing with their every word. However as peer workers we must never get hostile with people. We need to hone our skills in disagreeing with someone while respecting their opinions. Here is an example of a respectful disagreement. Friend: "Lets go bowling, I love it."

You: "I hate the bowling. It's for people who don't like a challenge. The halls are full of people I don't get on with."
You can see how this can escalate into an argument. It is defensive and judgemental. Consider this alternative.
Friend: "Lets go bowling, I love it."
You: "You're a big fan of social games. I never really got into it. Is there something else we could do?"

This is a very different approach.

We have stayed positive about their enjoyment of bowling' offered an alternative while being non-judgemental. Ask the group to think of times when they could have respected differences and had a positive disagreement.

What could they have changed?
Would the outcome have been different?
Is there someone they could use this skill with at the moment?
Think of how and when they could have used this skill in the past. Ask them to write in their workbooks what the situation was, how they could have done things differently and what the different outcomes may have been.

Respectful recovery interactions

- Work from strengths.
- Be fully present.
- Use open-ended questions.
- Be an effective listener.
- Respect differences.
- Remind them that they are the expert.
- Honour peoples choices.

<u>**Notes**</u>

DAY THREE

As with every other day on this course you should start by creating a discussion regarding what has gone before. Talk a little about how we now interact with people using recovery interactions. You should let individuals know how you have seen them progress so far. Recognise people's strengths in the room. This day is aimed at looking at diversity and environment.

A step in the right direction

We have covered a lot of ground and worked on some of the essentials of peer support. Now it is time to for you to see how far you have come already. Remember our supportive exercise where you were all assessed. Let's have another go! This time you should refer to the work we have been doing. Have your workbooks close at hand and take your time to get it right.

Exercise 30 minutes

In the same groups of three we will revisit the role-playing exercise.

One person will act as the peer support specialist: another will be receiving support while the third makes some specific notes on their observations. Each will take a turn at each role. The person observing needs to neutral throughout. Remember this may be the first time someone has been put in the position of supporting another. To this end our overall objective is to highlight the person's strengths, this is a major stepping-stone. As a peer support specialist you will utilise this tool extensively throughout your work practice. It is important that you practice and reflect upon your own strengths regularly and extensively.

Scene one
Peter has been supporting John over six months. It is Wednesday morning and as has been arranged, Peter is visiting John at home. John has just learned that he has not been accepted on a college course. He has been working towards it for the past year. He becomes tearful and says that he has missed out on all of his opportunities because of health problems. What differences did you note from the first time you tried this exercise?

After this exercise you should get everyone to feedback in front of the whole group.
Everyone should be more at ease with presenting in front of the whole group now.

"If man is to survive, he will have learned to take a delight in the essential differences between men and between cultures. He will learn that differences in ideas and attitudes are a delight, part of life's exciting variety, not something to fear."

As cited by Susan Sackett, author of "Inside Trek: A Star Trek Memoir", *-Gene Roddenberry,*

Recovery environment
Peer support specialists practice and develop skills that others in the mental health field may not necessarily utilise. Our direction and purpose are based in becoming

"An expert at not being an expert"

This may seem like a contradiction in terms, or worse, we are demeaning our role as something without merit. This is very far from the case. You have something to offer that no academic qualification can ever replicate or come close to; a lived experience that generates empathy and understanding. When we are in need of any other services we expect them to be experts by profession, lets face it none of us would put our lives in the hands of a pilot who didn't hold a pilots license, or a GP who had never qualified. All recovery is based in accepting and respecting the beliefs and cultures of others, to this end we need not necessarily be knowledgeable academically on the topic but we can interact mutually with a curiosity and awareness that lets the person know we respect their choices. If a person is seen only as suffering from a medical illness then these aspects of their lives can be disregarded by professionals as they are seen as unimportant in relation to the thing they are trying to treat, i.e. a psychotic episode or schizophrenia. We recognise and respect cultural diversity, religious beliefs, sexual orientation and many other facets in a person's life.

"If people are the building bricks of recovery then the cornerstone must be Self".

Ron Coleman, Recovery an alien concept.

Who are you?

As a group you have already looked at "who am I?" Now you will look at the diversity that people bring to the room. The next exercise should be fun. You should get people up on their feet and mingling for a good half an hour. Now that we have all spent a few days with each other we will all have greater understanding of our personal boundaries and learned how to interact mutually and respectfully with each other.

This next exercise will help us to take our relationships to a new level.
We will open up to who we are and the immense diversity that lies within the group and more importantly within ourselves. Below is a grid of sixteen different skills or attributes that someone may hold. The group should take fifteen minutes to find and cross of as many as possible.

The rules are simple.

1) You may only ask each person one question, they cannot guide or influence the question you ask.

2) If they do not fulfil the skill or attribute you have asked, then you must move onto someone else.

3) You may return to the same person after you have covered everyone else in the room.

GOOD LUCK!

climbed a mountain	speaks another language	born by the sea	has a sister
Meditates	Has been to America	related to twins	had surgery
prays often	believes in reincarnation	writes poetry	has a degree
lived abroad	owns animals	started a group	a connection with Judaism

Ask the trainees to provide a brief description of authentic selves within their workbook. Not the roles they perform, i.e brother, sister, worker etc but rather the person they know that they are under all the masks and roles that sway them away from their authentic selves.

The next exercise should turn into a wide-ranging discussion.
Top Tip
Your main objective is to steer the discussion towards how people who use services are worked with and how this can be changed.

It is worthwhile allowing the discussion to flow. You will find that the trainees' start speaking about how the service they work with treats and interacts with people. Again this is a chance to role model recovery. The group will come to their own conclusions about how to take service provision forward. This should take up to anything up to two hours.

Diversity

One of the major difficulties for all of us is to accept, recognise and celebrate the diversity that we each hold within. In being able to create an environment where recovery can blossom we need to role model acceptance of diversity. It is not our position to heal or cure or fix others, our role is in creating the environment where people feel safe enough and confident enough to share their own experiences and then begin the journey of re-claiming their own lives. Lets imagine that all the people close to you believe you will be ill for life. You will take medication all your days. That you should limit your job options to positions that require minimal effort as you may relapse at any time. They are constantly assessing your behaviour as you may become erratic. They are walking on eggshells; carefully choosing topics that they hope don't upset you. Everyone believes that to live a fulfilling life you will need support constantly. In their workbooks please ask trainees to take ten minutes to note down some of the things about themselves that they haven't taken into consideration and some things they have taken for granted. Think of their strengths that they have overlooked and celebrate the gifts that they hold within.

Some things you should know about me before you jump to conclusions.

Now as a group we will discuss whether these things are taken into consideration when people are using mental health services. What are the things about a person that should be taken into account?

What are the things about a person that should not be taken into account?

"Every man's ability may be strengthened or increased by culture." Abbott, John

Culture

This is where Peer support workers can really thrive. We don't work in the medical or maintenance models. We work in the process of recovery. A big part of this process is the environment that it takes place in. If we can get the environment right then the process of recovery can start to take place. In our own environments, away from this room we are all part of a wider community. Our communities are built on different cultures, values, attitudes, believes, histories and expectations. Our own identities are intrinsically woven around our environments and the boundaries that they carry. This can be a big challenge for some people as their beliefs are not necessarily those of the community within which they live. This can result in exclusion through stigma and discrimination. Or worse still a medical label that compounds the situation. During the day we integrate with many different environments all of which are made up of people from many different cultures. For instance in this room we are in a learning environment made up of people from different parts of the country. We will all be of different age, sex, religion and colour and this only enhances our learning experience. We have come together as a community of people with a shared interest and goal, specifically to qualify as peer workers. As we have seen from the exercise earlier, it can be difficult to discover specific things that contribute to a person's identity.

However in an environment conducive to recovery these attributes are brought to the fore. As a peer worker we accept differences and furthermore we celebrate them. Take ten minutes to fill in this cultural self-form in your workbooks.

1) Where I currently live
2) Where I was born
3) Five things that occurred during my life that have greatly influenced who I am.
4) The ethnic group I belong to.
5) What other groups I belong to.
6) My religious identification is.
7) My gender identification.

All of these headings or titles that we may give ourselves have been used to reduce a person to nothing more than a set of behaviours or patterns. Our role is not to work with these sub sets but to recognise and accept the differences in others. Let us now look at how, in this learning environment all of our cultural selves fit together as a community.

Our community
Let's piece together who we are as a community based on the addition of our cultures. Again ask people to write in their workbooks

Our Environment:

As we interact within this learning community we are continually influenced and steered by the overall environment. This may be like the physical set up of the premises, or more likely less tangible things like how we interact with each other. When we covered the environment for peer support on day one, we should see and feel the influence of that on day three. We should also notice the difference in language and now that we are getting to know each other our boundaries will have adapted to let the people we trust, in more. The values of a recovery environment are listed below, we will touch upon some of them and discover if we have created these elements within our community.

Environment for recovery

1) Core belief of team members
2) Interdependence
3) Self determination
4) Social inclusion.
5) High expectations
6) Responsibility
7) Holistic model

8) Social networks.
9) Choice.
10) Positive risk taking
11) Rights and advocacy

The aim of this exercise is to highlight how as a group you have created a recovery environment. The trainees will understand the main recovery threads that have ran through the week so far. You should point out how you have used recovery language, how you have kept the room safe during times of privacy and personal disclosure, how the agreement has evolved, how you have used open ended questions and reflective listening skills. This is the time on the course when the trainees see the potential to change how their services operate. It is essential that you create discussions on how they can help their own services evolve when they return after this week.
Now as a group we will discuss how these parts of a recovery environment are utilised within our learning community. (3/4 Hour)
Do you think that the environment has changed from day 1?

Ask them to use the space in their workbooks to highlight some of the areas they think have developed in terms or environment.

Forbes, Malcolm S.

We have looked at how culture, community and environment are interwoven and how they impact upon each other. We are now going to explore how the personal differences and the diversities we bring can add to and encourage our recovery environment. Each of us brings our own diversity to the group and no one is more or less correct than anyone else. As a peer worker we look at the bigger picture, we honour our own outlooks and the person's outlooks that we are working with. This creates an interwoven outlook. This new outlook is the guiding path that strengthens our relationship. It gives us the confidence and insight to learn from others and it instils confidence in others about us. This new outlook is a peer support workers vision tool. We can now relate to the persons experiences empathetically and honestly. This allows us not to be overbearing with our viewpoint and also not to be overridden by someone else's viewpoint. The new outlook that we generate allows the person to open up and begin the process of remembering who they are. Some people may have been using services for many years without ever really being allowed to air their view.

Day 4

As with other days you should start a discussion on what has gone before. Speak about cultural identity, use of environment, their sense of self, diversity. There should be some real changes taking place with regard to how people are interacting. You should highlight and recognise peoples' strengths in being able to embrace recovery.

At some point today you will need to go into detail about what is expected tomorrow.

This exercise is related to lots of what has taken place during the week. The objective is that the trainees understand that they can develop and learn from the people they work with, rather than always being the person in the know.

New outlook Exercise (40 minutes)
Take twenty minutes working in groups.

1) Consider a view that you brought to the table.

2) The view that others had around the table.
3) What the resulting new view looked like. We will then get back into our bigger group and discuss what we came up with.

1) The view I brought
2) The view that others had.
3) The new outlook

The trainees have covered a lot of ground so far and it is good practice to recognise the effort put in. However now it is time for them to start working in a recovery orientated way. Almost out of the blue you should get everyone on to their feet, explain that they will now take some time to appreciate each other. The rules are simple. They should use up as much available floor-space as possible, perhaps even using the grounds outside. They have one hour to go around everyone and tell each one what strengths they have seen in them during the week and why they appreciate them.

This is a very effectual exercise.

You should ask them when they have completed the exercise whether they would have acted and said the same things at the start of the course.

A big mistake!!!!

When meeting someone for the first time a big mistake we can all be guilty of is that of making assumptions. Taking this further, at times relationships we have been in for quite some time can be overran by assumptions. We think we automatically know what someone's responses and actions might be. As we have already seen this is the antithesis of a recovery environment. On the contrary it fosters maintenance. One of the best ways of honouring cultural diversity is to let the person tell you who they are. Remember, in mental health services people can be moved from one institution to another over many years. However their historical notes follow them and these can be a breeding ground for people building assumptions.

True or false (5 minutes) ask them to answer in the workbooks
If you encounter someone whose cultural identity holds a trait that you believe is detrimental to their recovery it is your job to change them and inform them of how the action is influencing them?
If a person tells you that some aspect of their culture is having a negative impact on them, your role is to find a solution and highlight alternatives.
Explain your answer in the workbooks

"In theory there is no difference between theory and practice. In practice there is."

Berra, Yogi

Diversity practice (1 hour)

Now that we have covered environment, culture, community and honouring diversity lets have a look at how we would react in some work situations. You will break up into smaller groups and discuss how to create the environment for recovery in the following scenes.

1) Dawn has been in hospital for six years. Only recently she gained a tenancy for her own flat, where she receives support from multifarious services. Dawns CPN is a practicing catholic. Dawn visited chapel every week before going into hospital. She tells you that her CPN has invited her to go along with her to the chapel she uses. Dawn asks you to accompany her as she feels comfortable in your company.

How would you respond?

2) Shaun has just started using the services that your organisation provides. One of the ideologies of Shaun's religion is that abortion is wrong. As you work with Shaun he expresses this view to you and tries to get you to agree that it is wrong.

How would you respond?

3) You are in the office when Steven, a co-worker reacts angrily to a news report. The report states that psychosis is on the in young people because of the increased

use of marijuana. Steven asserts that as marijuana is a natural stimulant it can't be responsible.

How would you respond?

A further step

We have covered a lot of ground and worked on some of the essentials of peer support. Now it is time to for you to see how far you have come already. Remember our supportive exercise where we were all assessed. Let's have another go! This time you should refer to the work we have been doing. Have your workbooks close at hand and take your time to get it right.

Exercise (30minutes)

In groups of three we will read a short role-playing exercise.
One person will act as the peer support specialist: another will be receiving support while the third makes some specific notes on their observations. Repeat this exercise so all 3 of you play each role. The person observing needs to stay neutral throughout. Remember this may be the first time someone has been put in the position of supporting another. To this end our overall objective is to highlight the person's strengths, this is a major stepping-stone. As a peer support specialist you will utilise this tool

extensively throughout your work practice. It is important that you practice and reflect upon your own strengths regularly and extensively.

Scene one

Peter has been supporting John over six months. It is Wednesday morning and as has been arranged, Peter is visiting John at home. John has just learned that he has not been accepted on a college course. He has been working towards it for the past year. He becomes tearful and says that he has missed out on all of his opportunities because of health problems. What has changed in your practice?

"People who wait for changes to occur on the outside before they commit to making changes on the inside will never make any changes at all."

Unknown, Source

We have come a long way, and covered a lot of ground this week. Most of the skills we have learned are founded in creating the environment for recovery to take place and then following that up through recovery practice. As a peer worker you will go on after this week and develop these skills. This is achieved through practice and awareness. There is however one major development that we have still to explore and that is Self. If you are not continuously modeling recovery and practicing the ethos then your work will reflect this.

Peer workers role model recovery.

The reason is quite simple. Peer workers are proof in the workplace that recovery happens. We have all had life experiences that brought us to this point and now we want to utilise that in a positive way. To help others construct and walk on their recovery journeys. Now that we have covered the basics it is time to move onto skill development. One of the greatest skills to develop is looking after your own well-being. This is not just about using coping techniques but rather about growing and developing alongside the people you work with. Every time we work with someone new we embark on a new and unique journey alongside the people we work with. To do this to the best of our abilities we ourselves need to feel well and confident in our abilities. This can take a lot of self-reflection.

"Self-love is not so vile a sin as self-neglecting."

Shakespeare, William

Why do I react the way I do to given situations?

How can I stay neutral?

What mask am I wearing today, and why?

Is this the right choice for me?

When we can ask and answer these questions openly and honestly, we further instill recovery around us. The people you work with will gain great confidence in you. As workers in recovery we spend some time looking for who we really are. This can become a battle of wits with our selves. Sometimes we can put a lot of effort into hiding who we really are for fear of failure or rejection.

When we begin to re-connect to ourselves it can be a real healing experience. We start to undertake new challenges and put ourselves in positions that we may not have before this self-acceptance.Do you ever feel disconnected from yourself, and how does it feel? Write the answers in your work book.Do you ever feel completely connected to yourself, and how does it feel?What benefits are there to staying connected to our authentic selves?

How can it benefit us in relationships with others?

How can you stay connected to your true self?

Barriers to self

There are many barriers that get in the way of connecting to our authentic selves. Some are obvious while others need some working out. How many of us are being true to our selves in this room? People may feel it is difficult to express an opinion for fear of ridicule. What barriers, if any do you feel at the moment? Ask group to shout them out

Our challenge, if we choose to accept it, is to find ways of negating and tearing down these self constructed barriers. This is no easy task. Many of us will have invested a lot of time and effort constructing these hideaways, and it may be an emotional journey tearing them down or just having a peek over their top. However to be a proficient peer support worker we must always recognise that recovery starts with self. The main function of these barriers has been to protect us. Protect us from perceived failure, ridicule or sometimes success.

Why would we protect ourselves from success? Again ask the group to shout out reasons

Over the years of creating these protective barriers, we have forgotten who our authentic self is! At some point they were constructive barriers but now they may just be a way of life. What are some of the ways in which you keep yourself from creating a connection to your authentic self? Again ask group to shout out answers and record on the flip chart

What reason do you have for sustaining these barriers? record on flip chart

When we look at our own barriers we can see the difficulty involved in being honest with ourselves about why we have them and how we can lower them. Now think of trying to deal with these barriers while experiencing a mental health problem or an addiction. For someone who has used services for many years some of these barriers have helped them through the system and served their purpose of protection and self-preservation. Unfortunately people who have used services for many years may have not been afforded the space that enhances development. To this end people can be stuck in a developmental phase that proves difficult to overcome. Their lives have become service dominated and the expectations of others compounds on their own view of themselves. Split into groups and discuss

1) What barriers people may have erected and why.
2) What are the developmental processes that people may have missed out on when using services?
3) What will then happen when they leave services?

Just as experiencing a mental health problem can get in the way of us connecting to our true selves, at times it can also force us into getting in contact with ourselves. Think of a time when an

experience steered you towards getting
more connected to self. Discuss with the
group

DAY 5

This final day is a celebration of the work undertaken by the trainees during the week. People will feel exhausted but also elated. The aim of this day is for the trainees to show how they can now role model recovery. Start the day by covering what has gone before and updating the working agreement if need be.

Presentations

One of the key skills of peer workers is being able to connect with the person. We have various tools at our disposal to accomplish this. One of which is being able to empathize honestly. To this extent the trainees should now be comfortable telling some of their life story.

That is what they will now demonstrate.

Everyone should present to the rest of the group for no more than five minutes on their own narrative.

TOP TIP these presentations need to be timed. You should ask someone to time how long they have been speaking for. At the four- minute mark they should hold up a sign saying one minute left. This lets the person know they have to start finishing up.

When a person has finished presenting you should ask them if they are open to questions or feedback.

Again you have another opportunity to role model recovery.

Acknowledge the persons strengths and empathize with their story.

Sharing our Gifts

In the notebooks everyone received on day one we will all right in a gift that the person brought to the week.

For instance

"Ann I would like to thank you for the gift of humour you have brought to this week. You have helped me to relax and enjoy this wonderful experience and I thank you for it."

People should pass around the notebooks being careful not to give it to whomever it belongs to. When they are complete you should hold onto them.

Short test

The trainees will now undertake a short test of twelve questions. As the trainer you should feel free to create different questions to the ones we have posed. The aim of this test is to check in that everyone has understood the content of the course. You will need to mark these during the lunch hour. When marking the tests you should note beside the answers how the person has grasped the concepts of the week.

The trainees should write their answers in their notebooks; this is when they will receive the gifts that people gave them.

You will find our final day feedback sheet on the accompanying CD.

Role- playing exercise

This is the final time the trainees will undertake this exercise that is why we refer back to the original exercise on day two.

The aim of this is to highlight the differences between how they supported each other on day one compared to today.

The big difference is that they will undertake the role playing in front of the rest of the group and get general feedback from the collective.

Exercise (1hour)
In pairs you will undertake a short role-playing exercise. Try out a respectful and dignified interaction, focussing in on a time in your life where you faced some challenge. One person will act as the peer support specialist. Each will take a turn at each role, the people observing need to remain neutral throughout. Remember this may be the first time someone has been put in the position of supporting another. To this end our overall objective is to highlight the peer workers strengths, this is a major stepping stone. As a peer support specialist we will utilise the art of building a persons self- esteem by recognition of their strengths and gifts extensively throughout your work practice. It is important that you practice and reflect upon your own strengths regularly and extensively as well.

Scene one

You have been receiving support for over six months. It is Wednesday morning and as has been arranged, your worker is visiting you at home. Think of a time when you faced a challenge and could have used support For instance maybe losing a job or a break up in a relationship. Explain to your worker what has happened.

After the role-playing exercise you should hand back all the marked notebooks. Use the rest of the afternoon to discuss how the trainees can take what they have learned on the course into the workplace.

Finally ask every one to stand in a circle, congratulate people on their hard work.
Ask people if they wish to give a last comment on the week, leave something behind in the middle of the circle and say their goodbyes, finish with a group hug or similar.